"Peter Arthur-Smith has written a lively, well *that is devoid of jargon and psychobabble. You do* *this simple blueprint for effective decision-making* *..... rationale* *for Option Solving is clearly illustrated and easy to follow. Smart Decisions adds an important arrow to the quiver of 21st century business leaders and guides them to making well-targeted choices."*

Georgette F. Bennett, Ph.D., President and Founder of **The Tanenbaum Center**, and author of "Crime Warps."

"By showing how to tap into the collective wisdom of an organization's workforce, Option Solving revolutionizes the way businesses make key decisions. Every entrepreneur and executive should read this book."

Professor Edward Rogoff, Chair, Department of Management, **Zicklin School of Business**, Baruch College, CUNY.

"In today's volatile environment, business development can be frozen by perceived problems and risks. Traditional business thinking simply leads to more paralysis by analysis. "Option Solving" is a breakthrough approach that gives you the theoretical framework, as well as productive processes and techniques, to reposition and further develop your business."

Raymond P. Ebeling, CEO, **American Shipping and Logistics Group**, current Chairman of National Defense Transportation Association, and recipient Admiral of the Ocean Seas Award (2004).

"Smart Decisions is a valuable guide to opportunity-finding. It retrains executives to value their intuition and give it a vital place beside their rational mind in making key decisions."

Anthony P. Rescigno, President, Greater New Haven Chamber of Commerce

SMART DECISIONS

GOODBYE PROBLEMS, HELLO OPTIONS

SMART DECISIONS

GOODBYE PROBLEMS, HELLO OPTIONS

By Peter A. Arthur-Smith

Published by Advantage, Charleston, South Carolina.
Member of Advantage Media Group.

ADVANTAGE is a registered trademark and the Advantage colophon is a trademark of Advantage Media Group, Inc.

Printed in the United States of America.

ISBN: 978-1-59932-162-2
LCCN: 2009938575

This publication is designed to provide accurate and authoritative information in regard to the subject matter covered. It is sold with the understanding that the publisher is not engaged in rendering legal, accounting, or other professional services. If legal advice or other expert assistance is required, the services of a competent professional person should be sought.

Most Advantage Media Group titles are available at special quantity discounts for bulk purchases for sales promotions, premiums, fundraising, and educational use. Special versions or book excerpts can also be created to fit specific needs.

For more information, please write: Special Markets, Advantage Media Group, P.O. Box 272, Charleston, SC 29402 or call 1.866.775.1696.

Visit us online at **advantagefamily**.com

Table of Contents

Acknowledgements

It is extremely important to me as a first-time writer to acknowledge how lucky I am to have so many people around me who have constantly challenged and brought me to this point. Some, like my family (Linda, my wife, and Amelia, Miranda, Robin and Simon) sometimes have had to watch from afar as I worked through these ideas and became engrossed in issues outside their daily lives. A better admission is that there have been several occasions when I have dragged Linda into the book process for her candid opinion, which I have done my best to listen to. I am so grateful for their forbearance, patience and emotional support that has made a work like this possible.

My immediate colleagues – Andrew, Chris, Denise, Jeff, Olger and Sheila – have been willing to contribute whenever asked. Some of them challenge me all the way to the bank, even when I don't ask! Without these colleagues, many of the ideas about Option Solving would never have crystallized as they have. I include Pat, of course, who helped more than once with word-processing the manuscript and who always met my need for changes and enhancements with her special sense of humor and personal stories.

My able board of advisers, Al, Bettye, Ed, Georgette, Howard, Joan and John – all so talented and experienced in their own right – have been especially long-suffering over the years, since they knew a book was important from the outset. Now they can be content that this will be one of a series where their input will always be welcome.

I also would like to acknowledge my many clients past and present who have allowed some of my experiences and thoughts to brew. Some have retired, much to the loss of the business world that has valued their fine minds and experience, and others still challenge me daily. I look forward to that continuing forever.

So many friends, some of them former clients, continue to enrich my life and are always willing to give input on my ideas. They and the others I've mentioned have contributed much to the content of this book. So perhaps it's *our* book rather than *my* book.

Finally, my career would never have taken the course it has without one particular mentor, Hakan E., a distinctly private person who has influenced so many business lives, including mine, but continues to work behind the scenes. Without him, I would not be as far along as I think I am. Thanks, Hakan.

Introduction

A Crisis in Decision Making

"The intuitive mind is a sacred gift; the rational mind is a faithful servant. We have created a society that honors the servant but has forgotten the gift." - Albert Einstein

The 2008-09 economic downturn called into question many of the business decisions that bankers, real estate executives, and many others had made. Folks on the street shook their heads in despair.

But what was disrupting so many lives was not just a world economic crisis; it was also a crisis in the art of decision making. We put executives at the helm and pay them so handsomely because they are supposed to have better judgment than those they lead. Their judgment determines the prosperity of both the company and their people – and when they make a plethora of bad decisions, they bolster the belief that they are paid too much.

The worldwide economic crisis was also a crisis in the art of decision making.

Albert Einstein despaired for a society that seemed to have turned away from intuitive thinking. Today's world seems even more rationally based than in his day. Everything seems to be based on numbers, whether business, sports, the news, the weather report, or academics.

We have become a society ever more obsessed with measurement, as reflected in the business and public administration programs of the last half-century. And we have become steeped in problem solving. We label our challenges as problems, giving them a negative connotation from the start, and tackle them with the logic of mathematicians and scientists. We survey. We study. We look for the rational solution. And we seem unable to move forward. It's paralysis by analysis.

The rational mind is focused on the numbers, the words, the logical, the tangible, the processes, the procedures, the sequential. But we also have intuitive minds that are creative, imaginative, conceptual, instinctive, interpretive.

In his research into epilepsy in the early 1960s, Dr. Roger Sperry of the California Institute of Technology found that when the brain's left and right hemispheres were separated, the left brain couldn't distinguish truth from fiction. The brain's left hemisphere is the rational one; the right side is more intuitive. What this key finding shows us is

Strict rationality limits us in so many ways – and our businesses and organizations, too.

that we require our intuitive minds to make the best judgments. For questions of complexity, the right brain is more likely to give the best answers.

And yet we have based our schooling system on the left brain. Problem solving is a steady diet of so many academic disciplines; young people are conditioned to it and find it perpetuated in their careers. Those who support the rational approach will point to good conclusions derived from gathering data and using logic. But such strict rationality limits us. In so many ways, it holds us back – and our organizations and businesses, too.

When one examines our rational, logical conclusions, they are based purely upon man-made systems. Scholastic aptitude tests, for example, present arithmetic and formulas that lead to predetermined, logical answers. If we follow all the right steps and make the right logical calculations, we get the right answers. We exercise the left-brain "muscle." Those who work hard at developing that muscle, or who are naturally endowed, do well on the tests. Others who may have great intuitive minds are pushed to the sidelines – particularly if they are from less-affluent families and haven't developed impressive vocabularies, a left-brain trait.

In the 20th century, the growth in the science of economics has pushed us deeper and deeper into formulas, problems, and rational solutions. Mathematicians are increasingly in demand, especially in banking and investment. In financial trading programs, computers make the deals when market data, fed into formulas, trigger buys and sells. This is what the world has come to – and it's the approach that created the 2008-09 fiscal crisis. It has been pretty well devoid of intuitive judgment.

In our work and personal lives, we are beset by problems that we have been trained since childhood to solve logically and rationally. Life brings us experiences that equip us to use our minds, yet we are stifled from using them. Nature gives us the tool to realize the full benefits of our intuitive nature, but we are blindsided from using it. Yet if we could fully draw upon this innate capability, we could access a realm of possibilities in better solving our professional and life issues.

Sometimes what counts cannot be counted, Einstein also said, and what can be counted doesn't count. The enormous potential of the human mind and its possibilities cannot be measured with SATs.

How tall or heavy someone is, while interesting, doesn't often count in the scheme of things. A business person's penchant for figuring financials to the last penny does not really count, except perhaps for tax purposes. Rather, what matters is the ability to invest financial resources in the right opportunity.

Before the financial crisis, many intuitive thinkers questioned the judgments of our business and organizational leaders. Here are some examples:

- The auto industry: As General Motors, Ford, Chrysler and others were pumping out SUVs and flashy gas guzzlers, some people remembered prior energy crises and suggested the oil market could soon show us the insanity of such behavior. In 2008, it did.

- The real estate industry: As prices soared in the home and commercial building markets, those who had experienced the1987-1990 real estate collapse, or who remembered Japan's problems in the mid-1990s, were asking, "When is the bubble going to burst?" In 2008, it did.

- The financial industry: As banks enticed so many to pursue credit-card debt and promoted equity loans, and as bankers and investment executives received obscene bonuses, there were those who wondered, based on prior market downturns: "When will people be loaded up with more debt than they can handle?" In 2008, it all collapsed.

- Government: As the politicians went on a spending spree using the boom in tax revenue, some who had seen plenty of booms and busts wondered when such behavior would catch up with us. Then, in 2008-09, came major layoffs of police, firefighters, teachers – people essential to society's well being. It caught up with us.

Why did industry and government get it wrong? After all, they have their fair share of smart people. It's because they trusted the numbers and their attractive formulas and snazzy problem solving kits. They drew their rational conclusions. They thought they were on to a winner.

It's as Dr. Sperry concluded in his experiments: The left brain cannot tell truth from fiction.

Had these captains and henchmen of industry and government relied more on intuition, they probably would have come to different conclusions – provided they understood what was going on. Yes, research is important. We need our left brains. As Einstein pointed out, the rational mind is a faithful servant. Its job is to do the digging so that it can pose the right questions to the intuitive mind. But it's the intuitive mind, with its ability to synthesize complexities and lighter shades of gray, which has the "sacred gift" for making the most effective judgments.

It's a delicate balance. We need both our rational and intuitive minds to draw whole-mind conclusions. Unless their roles are put into proper perspective, we are more than likely to make the wrong judgments. No matter how powerful we think our rational mind is, we should not rely on it to make judgments. We only need it to be the servant that poses the questions to our intuitive minds, our sacred gift.

When leaders rely so much on their rational minds
to make decisions, when they focus on "problems,"
we are led into crisis.

When leaders rely so much on their rational minds to make decisions, when they focus on "problems," we are led into crisis – as illustrated by the economic collapse. The more classical their education, the more they are steeped in such behavior. They become enamored of the slam-dunk of the numbers. Lost in their problem solving processes, they overrule their instincts.

We have long failed to take advantage of our intuitive gift and its power over our rational, servant mind, as Daniel Pink points out in his book *Whole New Mind* (Penguin Books, 2005). Yet it's the intuitive mind that gets us to work safely every day, that keeps us out of trouble in personal relationships, that enables us to detect danger and allows us to enjoy so much around us. We take for granted this extraordinary human resource and treat it as ordinary –who cares, we say, so long as the numbers are there?

Look at the world of economics. In a letter to *The New York Times* in March 2009, George Cooper, author of *The Origin of Financial Crises: Central Banks, Credit Bubbles and the Efficient Market Fallacy*, had this to say: "While the details of each cycle differ, the core processes remain constant…. Asset inflation and credit creation form a …'virtuous cycle' that drives both asset prices and debt stock to unsustainable levels. Then comes the Minsky moment (named after Hyman Minsky, economist) when the virtuous cycle flips into a vicious one of credit contraction and asset deflation."

Is it possible that this flip comes when intuition finally overpowers the "numbers headlights" that shine into the eyes of the rational thinkers? Even though we've had lessons from history, we still do things the same way. Should we overhaul the way we make economic and business decisions?

There's a reason we go through these miserable "booms and busts" in our world. Despite the fact that our rational mind cannot tell truth from fiction, we still allow ourselves to be sold on the numbers – the logical, rational outcome. Our parents educated us that way, our schools and universities educated us that way, our employers educated us that way, and our governments educated us that way. We have become a society that loves a problem (especially a numerical one), despite the negative connotation associated with the word.

Wouldn't life be so much more interesting if we could focus instead on opportunities rather than problems? As one wise man said, "Problems are only carefully disguised opportunities."

As one wise man said, "Problems are only carefully disguised opportunities."

Perhaps this is why we have juvenile delinquents and dropouts. It may be what leads people to change jobs so often. Some of them may have extraordinarily intuitive minds that rebel at the rational conclusions of those in authority.

We must recognize our crisis in decision making and judgment. We must rethink our predilection toward problem solving. We must try a fresh approach that uses our whole mind and gives us much better results. We need to use the extraordinary gifts that nature has given us.

This fresh approach not only makes decisions more effectively, it involves more people in doing so, which is what we all crave. People prefer to be led, not managed. They want to feel involved rather than have the bosses do the thinking for them. They don't want to feel like robots – and when they do, they may seem to act like robots, or slaves.

If we can make this step, we can enjoy a much better quality of life than we might imagine. Let's take this road to discovery of our intuitive minds. Let's try option solving instead.

Chapter 1

The Whole Mind Approach

"Today, the defining skills of the previous era – the "left-brain" capabilities that powered the Information Age – are necessary but no longer sufficient. And the capabilities we once disdained or thought frivolous – the "right-brain" qualities of inventiveness, empathy, joyfulness, and meaning – increasingly will determine who flourishes and who flounders."
-Daniel Pink, A Whole New Mind *(Penguin Group, 2005)*

During the industrial age, we became preoccupied with management and created the tools to support its practices. Coupled with the capitalist focus on 'ownership,' which wanted full control over all business aspects, mechanisms were developed for planning, organizing, directing and controlling most businesses. Mechanisms like these would ensure that owners would have control over their initial investment and reap a healthy profit.

An incredible array of planning, analysis and reporting tools have emerged over the years to meet owners' control requirements.

An incredible array of planning, analysis and reporting tools has emerged over the years to meet owners' control requirements. They come from the left brain, the rational side, where things can be counted. For workers and their supervisors (who play a left-brain "inspection" role), these tools have become an ingrained habit.

Additionally, we have seen a tremendous growth in problem solving, encouraged by our parental and scholastic upbringing. We spend a tremendous amount of our time focusing on problems: political problems, economic problems, business problems, organizational problems, personal problems, family problems, and so on. The number of our problems seems endless, to the point where our whole lives are a problem.

No wonder we become depressed and morale falls in our businesses.

Good coaches and leaders focus on opportunities rather than problems, because in every problem they see a silver lining. Traditional managers focus on problems, giving them a feeling of greater personal control.

"Control" is largely a myth. There are so many things in business and in life that we cannot control.

But that "control" is largely a myth. There are so many things in business and in life that we cannot control. We have no more ability to control the forces of business and life than a surfer has to control the ocean. All one really can do is look for the next best wave to ride.

Similarly, business leaders should be looking for the next wave of opportunity to ride, rather than ways to control the current one.

They should be trying to ride the current wave as long as is practicable. Once they spot the next *right* business wave, they should ensure that they have the right product/service "surf board" and the right people to ride it as long as possible. However, they will only be able to spot the right business wave if they focus on *option* solving rather than *problem* solving.

As organizations grow larger, management works even harder at introducing rational and structured solutions, as well as efficiency, fine-tuning, problem analysis and accuracy. All these areas are taken care of by the left hemisphere of the brain, the rational side. Eventually such activities build into a bureaucratic boondoggle where it is virtually impossible to get anything done – just ask any congressman or senator. Such an emphasis on repetitive, problem solving, left-brain work seems to make workers tired, numb and unengaged. No wonder so many CEOs complain of their workforces being uninspired.

Now enter the right brain, the intuitive side, the side that has enormous spatial sense. Whereas the left brain, with its language facility, handles what is said, the right brain focuses on how it's said – the facial expression, tone of voice, circumstances in which it was said. The right brain assesses all these factors in an instant, checks them against experiences since childhood, and decides exactly how to respond. As was pointed out in a *New York Times* article in April 2007 titled "When the Group is Wise":

The left-brain, with its language facility, handles what is said. The right-brain focuses on how it's said – facial expression, tone of voice, circumstances in which it was said.

"Yet out in the world, no one uses questionnaires or diagnostic manuals to check out a stranger or an acquaintance. People read the other person's body language, tone of voice; they read between the lines of what is said. They absorb most of this information instantly, unconsciously, and often accurately, studies suggest."

Such intuitive attributes were developing way before the analytical and verbal skills of a person's left brain started to fully take shape. A person's intuitive side has watched events and heard noises since birth, or even in the womb. The verbal and rational side is honed from the time a child starts to verbalize. Schools exercise that left-brain muscle with math, language, science and reading, perhaps to get control over children's behavior and funnel them along designated career tracks and societal norms. Most scholastic tests such as SATs examine the mettle of the left-brain: As Peter Senge wrote in his book *Schools that Learn: A Fifth Discipline* (Doubleday/ Currency, 2000), "If we want to change schools, it is unlikely to happen until we understand more deeply the core assumptions on which the industrial-age school is based."

Leaders can increase passion and commitment in their people by using intuitive tools, such as stories, examples, pictures, and exciting visions.

The right-brain muscle is able to mix and match colors, discern all sorts of shapes, imagine all sorts of different combinations, and anticipate what others are likely to say purely by their physical stance or facial expression. However, we judge people, more often than not, by their ability to articulate (their left-brain capability) rather than on their ability to size up situations or see fresh angles to situations (their right-brain capability). How many times have we met people who seem relatively inarticulate but who bring extraordinary, perceptive reactions to certain activities? People like chefs, musicians, artists and designers may not be especially articulate but can be enormously creative and imaginative, to the benefit of many.

Good leaders tend to rely on their intuitions (right-brain thinking) much more. They visualize the future, enjoy sizing up opportunities, and encourage their people to come up with creative solutions. They have the ability to raise the level of passion and commitment within their people purely by utilizing different intuitive tools – they give examples, tell stories, show interesting pictures, offer fun experiences, come up with exciting visions. Managers tend to rely on rational tools: plans, budgets, systems, policies, procedures, controls and compliance.

Author Daniel Pink sees the left brain as sequential, the right brain as simultaneous; the right hemisphere as providing the picture, the left as providing the thousand words. We can make better decisions by using these right-brain capabilities to our advantage.

Figure 1   <u>**RIGHT-BRAIN FOCUS: LEFT-BRAIN FOCUS**</u>

<u>KNOWN LEFT-BRAIN FEATURES</u>	<u>KNOWN RIGHT-BRAIN FEATURES</u>
• **Rational thinking**	• **Intuitive thinking**
• **Detail minded**	• **Conceptual minded**
• **Analytically oriented**	• **Synthesis oriented**
• **Sequential approach**	• **Simultaneous approach**
• **Creates what is said**	• **Interprets how it is said**
• **Research oriented**	• **Creativity oriented**
• **A thousand words**	• **The overall picture**
• **Brilliant (knows so much)**	• **Genius (the big idea)**

Leadership
Solutions, Inc.
Insightful Solutions for Effective Leadership Performance

Based on Daniel Pink's book - 'A Whole New Mind' (Penguin Group 2005) PLUS LSI's own experiential findings.

Our understanding of the enormous capabilities of the intuitive mind is expanding by the day. Dr. Roger Sperry, who won the 1981 Nobel Prize for medicine, showed through his research into epilepsy that when our left brains are completely disconnected from our right brains, we cannot tell truth from fiction. This strongly suggests that we cannot trust our left brains for making complex judgments, unless associated with man-made formulas that will produce an outcome based upon rational logic. It is far better that we make the fullest use of our right brains, which can synergize all the complexities involved in our day-to-day decision making.

Research suggests that we cannot trust our left brains
for making complex judgments.

A May 2008 article in *Natural History* by Marco Iacoboni, neu-rologist and neuroscientist at the David Geffen School of Medicine at the University of California, Los Angeles, discussed cells in our brains called mirror neurons: "Mirror neurons are incredibly powerful; 'vicarious' would not be a strong enough word to describe their effects." They enable us to anticipate other people's actions and re-enact their actions without even thinking about it. He also pointed out, "What do people really do all day, every day? We 'read' the world." And we don't even think about it. We take it for granted; an extraordinary gift seemingly taken to be so ordinary!

These revelations about human behavior point to the need for changing the way we make decisions. They call for new business leadership tools. We need to focus not on problem solving, a left-brain trait, but on option solving, a way to tap into people's extraordinary capabilities.

Option solving makes the best use of our intuitive nature. As we shall see, it asks the proper questions and frames them in a way that will engage the right brain's creativity. It encourages the examination of the overall picture and diverse choices. And because it considers a range of choices, option solving minimizes the human doubt that arises when the intuitive mind is restricted by traditional problem solving.

With option solving, the appropriate workforce groupings become far more engaged and involved, particularly when included in decision making. Even though people's left-brain capabilities (as so often exhibited by their ability to articulate their ideas) may not be especially pronounced, they still have extraordinary right-brain capabilities that are largely underutilized in today's business and organizational worlds. Option solving is one way to tap into these capabilities.

Now that computers do all the sequential, numerical and processing tasks, with far greater consistency and accuracy than humans, companies can free up their people to focus on their more imaginative, synthesizing and innovative capabilities that allow them to make the best decisions. Not only will this engage people's minds more, but it will also encourage them to be considerably more productive. They can stop focusing on the problems – and start assessing their options.

Questions for Consideration

- To what degree are your people going through the motions because of your company's left-brain emphasis?

- To what degree do your people utilize their enormous right-brain capacity to meet their personal needs rather than your company's needs?

- To what degree do you provide a work environment focusing on opportunities rather than problems?

- To what extent does your company have the right working principles to draw upon your people's enormous capabilities?

Chapter 2

Problem Solving vs. Option Solving

"We assume that the key to solving problems or making good decisions is finding that one right person who will have the answer.... We should stop hunting and ask the crowd (which, of course, includes the geniuses as well as everyone else) instead. Chances are, it knows."

-From "The Wisdom of Crowds," James Surowiecki

(Anchor Books, Random House, 2004/2005, introduction)

L et's take a look at some fundamental differences between problem solving, the traditional method of the rational world, and option solving, the whole-brain approach of intuitive thinkers.

Imagine the frustration of those workers who have solutions but cannot make well-articulated cases.

Figure 2   **IT'S OPTION SOLVING: NOT PROBLEM SOLVING**

PROBLEM SOLVING	OPTION SOLVING
• Logical, rational approach.	• Synthesis, intuitive approach.
• Few, limiting choices.	• Wide-ranging choices.
• Exclusive, few involved.	• Inclusive, many involved.
• Conservative outcomes.	• Imaginative possibilities.
• Focuses on rules.	• Sets consensus boundaries.
• Immediate option exclusion.	• Postpones option exclusion.
• Piecemeal approach	• Comprehensive approach
• Encourages inertia.	• Advances momentum.

Leadership Solutions, Inc.®
Insightful Solutions for Effective Leadership Performance

Logical, rational approach – compared with – synthesis, intuitive approach.

Traditional problem solving demands a clearly stated rationale that people hopefully grasp before anyone proceeds. In many cases, this expectation slows everything down because so many things cannot be explained in a rational and defined manner. Such outcomes also require the problem solvers to have the eloquence for convincing their colleagues. Just imagine the frustration of those workers who have solutions but cannot argue their case sufficiently. It is hardly surprising that so many of them give up and toe-the-line, while more loquacious players get their way.

Most workers are able to synthesize diverse factors and use intuitive instincts to sense solutions to fairly complex issues. The challenge for most executives is how to access that capability. It's there

– it surrounds them all the time – but it is underutilized. It's available when tapped at the right time and in the right manner.

What brings out this asset is a climate of trust and confidence in which less articulate workers feel comfortable to step up. They are particularly likely to do so in an option solving session, where the right options are revealed and they can "see" the choices. They will step forward when the right questions are asked. These questions usually begin with the words *what, who*, and *which*, as in, "What do you think can be our best option?" That asks for an opinion rather than a rational explanation, which is elicited by the other interrogatives: why, how, when, where.

Few, limiting choices – rather than – Wider-ranging choices.

In traditional problem solving, we often limit our thoughts to the most immediate alternatives: good or bad. Take the perennial problem of poorly performing employees. We generally think of our two main alternatives: demote or fire them.

In option solving, however, we develop a much wider range of options, such as: replace the person's manager, transfer the person to another area, provide some intense coaching, team the person with a strong role model, clarify motivational issues, and so on. We could well come up with a more creative solution, particularly if we corral the right group of advisers. And a good solution can save a big investment in time and money.

Exclusive, few involved – as opposed to – Inclusive, many involved.

By its nature, problem solving generally happens in a small group. Traditional managers too often tend to problem solve on their own. Their people sit back and let their manager do all the thinking. The one or two people involved in solving a problem will pursue their deliberations and look for rational solutions that then have to be explained to those who will implement the outcome. These managers often wonder why their solution is not embraced with great enthusiasm – and that's because their people, who so often will see things differently with their own intuitive perspectives, have not been sufficiently involved.

Option solving utilizes a wider number of participants, reaches a broader consensus, and allows for a greater amount of staff and worker involvement. Involvement is one of the bigger opportunities for companies in the 21ˢᵗ century. Today's more educated workforces expect to be involved. Their biggest beef is a lack of "communication" by their executives. When they complain about inadequate communication, workers are basically saying that they feel insufficiently involved. So when leaders hear the word *communication,* they can translate it as *involvement.* Executives cannot involve their people in everything, but there is still plenty of room for improvement. There is no shortcut to effective communication. If executives don't devote time to it now, they will pay the price later. The pay-off will be much greater engagement at all levels.

> *Today's educated workforces expect to be involved – and companies should see that as an opportunity.*

Option solving lets participants "buy in" to the outcome, by involving as many people as possible – and "buy-in" is a major desire of most executives. Participants have a chance to interpret the "picture" of alternatives and feel as if they are part of the outcome. (Note: The one thing that option solving facilitators will have to watch for is "The Herd

Mentality." See the book *Nudge* by Richard Thaler and Cass Sunstein, Penguin Books, 2008/2009. They will have to challenge participants to respect their own instincts and not just follow their colleagues.)

Conservative outcomes – as opposed to – Imaginative possibilities.

Traditional problem solving usually produces rational solutions that tend to lean toward the conservative (risk averse) because people are not given the scope to think outside the box. Consider the dilemma of a business school dean whose tenured faculty seems uninterested in creating a more enlightened curriculum. The dean feels he has two choices to present to his conservative-minded provost: either buy out the faculty, or forget about such changes. You can guess how the cash-strapped provost would choose.

However, suppose the dean requested an option solving session with a wider brainstorming audience, including the provost. The question before them would be: "What are our most creative options for handling lackadaisical tenured professors?" Besides the two choices already given, others might emerge, such as 1) challenging the faculty with fresh assignments; or 2) having the dean and provost talk about the possibilities with each faculty member who resists change; or 3) for professors who still resist, "putting them in the window," or setting them on the sidelines while others forge ahead with the new ideas.

Those are options that might never arise without an option solving session that includes a wider audience of thinkers. And that could be just what it takes to convince a conservative provost to buy into a more imaginative option.

Focuses on rules – rather than -- Sets consensus boundaries

Too often, traditional problem solving is bound by rules and protocol, either written or unwritten. Some of these rules include:

- Defer to the person with the most experience or authority.

- Don't proceed without a rational, conclusive solution.

- Don't accept a solution that's against current organizational wisdom.

- Don't suggest a solution from outside the organization.

- Don't proceed without more data and facts.

When it comes to option solving, there are only six principles:

- Ask the right question and frame the possibilities.

- Be imaginative and think "out of the box."

- Avoid asking "how, why, when or where" until the best option is identified.

- Avoid excluding any option until all options have emerged.

- Allow participants to support a less than conclusive option.

- Accept hunches or gut feelings.

Immediate option exclusion – instead of – Postpones option exclusion

When a traditional manager tries to solve a problem, either alone or in a small huddle, the "nix" principle often comes into play; that is, they quickly rule out any choice that may not have a rational solution. Consequently, their choices are limited, often to just one.

In option solving, however, no reasonable choice is excluded until all the possibilities have emerged. When you engage in option solving, you can make a less-than-conclusive choice because it seems to be what's best at the moment. Option solving assumes it is best not to eliminate anything until all the viable possibilities have emerged.

Piecemeal approach – rather than a – Comprehensive approach

Too often with traditional problem solving, different alternatives are considered at different times and within differing contexts. This loses the advantage of taking a comprehensive view within a certain window of time. Option solving, on the other hand, looks at all the alternatives at once, allowing them to be considered as a whole. It allows the right-brain intuitive mind to do its stuff.

Encourages inertia – compared with – Advances momentum

Problem solvers often postpone action until they can fully justify the outcome. They may demand an employee survey, or data-base analysis, or customer poll before a solution can be ratified. Oh boy!

Not that there is anything fundamentally wrong with such activities, but too often they just postpone action. The old ways allow the continuation of inertia, and the momentum of emotional support is lost.

> *Problem solvers tend to postpone action.*
> *They may demand a survey, or data-base analysis,*
> *or customer poll.*

Option solving, on the other hand, allows for solutions that are less than perfect to be suggested and acted upon if they are the best course of action at the time. If better options emerge later on, that's fine. They can be incorporated when the time comes. With such an approach, momentum builds while emotional support is strong. And that support can overcome the influence of naysayers who try to use logic to hold sway and get their way.

Questions for consideration

- To what degree do you involve your people today in problem solving or option solving?

- What importance do you give to perfection over building momentum when making decisions?

- To what degree do you try to "manage" your organization and do the entire problem solving yourself?

- In what ways do you believe option solving can help your workforce "buy into" solutions?

Chapter 3

Asking the Right Questions and Establishing Bookends

"Theory of Mind" [is] defined by cognitive scientists as humans' innate ability, evolved over millions of years, to judge others' changing thinking, their understandings, their intentions, their pretenses. It is a judgment faculty, quite different from our quantitative faculties."
-Robert J. Shiller, "It Pays to Understand the Mind-set"
New York Times, *March 2009*

Option solvers must start out by asking the right question and framing the possibilities. The question must get to the context of the issue at hand. Then, option solvers use what they call "bookends" to set the boundaries within which all viable solutions will be framed.

Let's use a simple example to show how it works:

Suppose a company is considering whether to replace a specific piece of equipment. This would be the contextual question: "Should we replace equipment *X* in our plant?" However, for company circumstantial reasons, we should broaden the question as used in Figure 3 (see also Chapter 5).

The bookends should be solutions considered to be unlikely because they are extremes. The eventual solution likely will fall between those extremes, so the bookends provide a framework for "nudging" the intuitive mind to come up with its most creative, viable options. In deciding what to do about the equipment, the option solvers might choose these as their bookends: 1) Keep using it as is, or 2) Don't replace it with anything.

Figure 3   **OPTION SOLVING : NOT PROBLEM SOLVING**

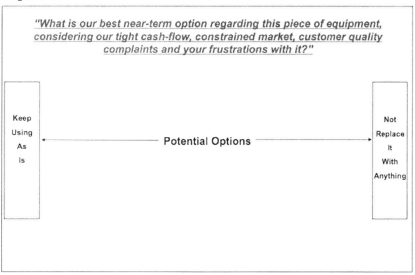

"What is our best near-term option regarding this piece of equipment, considering our tight cash-flow, constrained market, customer quality complaints and your frustrations with it?"

Keep Using As Is   ◄———— **Potential Options** ————►   Not Replace It With Anything

Leadership Solutions, Inc.

The company probably will not keep using troublesome equipment without even making repairs, nor will it refuse to replace even part of the equipment. The step of setting the bookends draws upon people's inclination to make comparisons, and the more provocative the bookends the better because they invite alternative ideas and stimulate the intuitive mind.

The eventual solution likely will fall between extremes – and defining those extremes provides the framework for "bookends" and helps stimulate the intuitive mind.

Asking the right contextual question is important, too. In this example, it seems obvious what the question should be. But in other cases, it's important not to make the question too restrictive. People must feel encouraged to think creatively. To tap into the right brain, it often helps to begin the contextual question with the word "what," which invites opinions and discourages, for the time being, too much talk about the details.

Also, there is every likelihood that the question won't be that obvious because of the issues involved in framing it. In such cases, some good positive debate can be used to hammer out a consensus question. One approach is to list all the key issues and then phrase a question accordingly. Once the right contextual question is in place –supported by the bookends – then everything else falls into place. It is therefore well-worth spending the time on it, although with a strongly intuitive rather than a rational approach. *(NOTE: For more on this, go to www. optionsolving.com.)*

Let's take another example. A company president wants his leadership team to become more engaged. He doesn't sense enough commitment or initiative from his team. Before considering his options, he establishes the question: "What's it going to take to get my leadership team more involved?" Then, working with his CEO and two outside advisers, he sets the bookends. (A wise leader doesn't try to resolve challenging issues alone, though this particular question does limit who joins the session. *Note: An April 2009 report in Fortune Small Business magazine revealed that 69 percent of women entrepreneurs are more likely to seek business advice, whereas only 47 percent of male entrepreneurs are likely to do the same.*)

Figure 4   **OPTION SOLVING : NOT PROBLEM SOLVING**

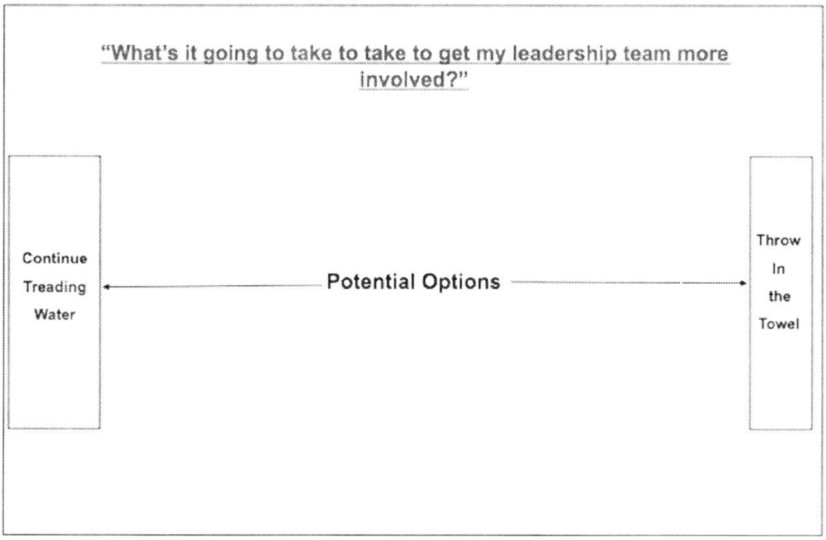

"What's it going to take to take to get my leadership team more involved?"

| Continue Treading Water | ←———— Potential Options ———— → | Throw In the Towel |

Leadership Solutions, Inc.

Here are the bookends they chose: 1) Keep the current team and tread water. 2) Throw in the towel and sell the company. The first option was untenable because the president had had enough of several members of his team, though not all of them. He felt he couldn't move forward without a change. And it was highly unlikely he would throw in the towel. But the choices were provocative. They were worst-case scenarios from which he had to step back.

Bookends should not be too obvious or tame. They should "nudge" the sensibilities, if possible. By doing so, they serve to stimulate the creative and imaginative right brain to do its stuff. They encourage the intuitive mind to show its mettle.

Questions for consideration

- What business or organization issues keep you awake at night?

- What challenging issue do you have facing your organization over the longer term?

- To deal with those issues, to what extent can you use option solving so that others can join you in developing solutions?

Chapter 4

Principles and Practices in Choosing Options

"In making every purchase decision, buyers implicitly weigh alternatives, often unconsciously…. The thought process is intuitive for individual consumers and industrial buyers alike."
-From Blue Ocean Strategy, *W. Chan Kim and Renée Mauborgne*
(Harvard Business School Press, 2005, pp. 49-50)

In the same way that consumers make their choices intuitively, for better or for worse, so do company leaders and staff. The latter, however, operate in an environment with which they are extremely familiar, for eight hours a day, five days a week, at least 48 weeks a year – and many years, at that. That makes their intuitions about work and market-related issues pretty reliable.

Option solving makes full use of a staff's experience and intuition, leading to better decision making and forward momentum.

Option solving is designed to channel those intuitions to the company's advantage, with better decision making and forward momentum. It avoids the delays caused by searching for ever better data to support rational decisions. To get the greatest value from such a fresh approach, it helps to define the principles and practices.

Option Solving Principles

- Ask the right contextual question and set up the right bookends. These are the features we discussed in Chapter 3.

- Allow people's imagination and out-of-the-box thinking to flow. The more innovative the exercise is allowed to be, the more people will value it.

- Avoid asking "how, why, when or where" questions until an option is chosen. Allowing such questions will likely switch people into their traditional rational thinking, discouraging the mind-rush of innovative ideas.

- Avoid excluding any option until all options have emerged. To encourage maximum creativity, at least five or six options should be drawn up before making any choices.

- Allow participants to choose a less than conclusive option. Option solving encourages realistic thinking and the trade-offs that have to be made (the intuitive mind is pretty good at doing this, whereas the rational mind finds it almost impossible to do). Sometimes there is no perfect option and the best available should be chosen. Perhaps better options will emerge as a situation unfolds, but at least progress will not have been put on hold and therefore encourage inertia.

- Accept hunches or gut feelings. Since option solving is intuitive, a choice based on a reasonable hunch is acceptable. There are numerous examples where hunches have proven correct. The important thing is that participants don't have to rationalize or explain their hunches. If they instinctively "feel" something is appropriate, that is sufficient and permissible: It makes full use of their intuitive capacity.

If there's no perfect option, choose the best available.
A better one may emerge, but at least progress
will have been made.

Option Solving Practices

- Once you have chosen a primary option, you can move on to sub-options. This is known as "peeling the onion." How it's done will be discussed in Chapter 7.

- The technique of "emotional distancing" helps participants get clarity once all options have been listed. It's particularly important when a lot of heavy thinking or emotionally sensitive options are in play. See Chapter 8.

- Phrasing the right option solving question stimulates the best result. It appears the intuitive left brain responds better to questions starting with *what, which,* or *who.*

- The bookend options should be as unlikely and provocative as possible. This, too, stimulates the intuitive senses to find alternatives.

- The bookends shouldn't be too obvious. This encourages creative thinking as participants look for solutions.

- Before considering a range of options, outline constraints and opportunities. These might include cost issues, market possibilities, people challenges, customer openings, etc. If participants know about them, their choices likely will be that much more appropriate.

- The option solving facilitator should look for signs that participants have exhausted their creative thoughts. They may look down, shake their heads, throw their heads back, and so on. These can signal, "I'm done."

- When working alone with option solving (most likely on personal matters), it is important not to start considering any options until at least five or six have been identified. It is much harder to discipline oneself to do this when working alone. However, overall results will show the extra value.

- Participants should anonymously indicate their preferred option on a folded piece of paper handed to the facilitator. This practice helps avoid the risk of a "herd mentality."

- Once an option has been chosen and the vote is over, it helps to note participants' reasons for their choice. This can help make everyone emotionally comfortable with the final choice.

- Facilitators should look for likely biases. If clear biases are allowed to creep into an option solving exercise, other participants will become dissatisfied with the outcome. See Chapter 9.

- Make sure participants are appropriately informed. If the group is insufficiently informed about pertinent factors of an issue, every effort should be made to brief them properly. It may be necessary for an expert to be present at the outset of a session to answer questions and share appropriate insights with participants.

- Option solving encourages "trade-offs" that are important in complex decisions. This will automatically happen as participants use their intuitions to frame their choices against the original question and seek alternatives.

These principles and practices allow option solvers the opportunity to use their "whole mind" and make the best judgments. Decisions will improve dramatically, as will company performance.

By using the "whole mind," option solvers make the best judgments, improving company performance.

Questions for consideration

- What do you see as the most important principles and practices listed above?

- Which of the listed principles and practices have the strongest appeal to you and will probably encourage you to pursue the option solving approach?

- What thoughts have you given to creating decision principles and practices in the past?

Chapter 5

First Option Solving Exercise

"… our intuition processes are somewhere between 1,000 and 10,000 times as fast as our rational mind. In addition, we know it synthesizes parts into a unified whole, generates creative energy in the process and also cannot be deceived."

- *From* Breaking the Rules, *Kurt Wright (CPM Publishing, 1998)*

As we've already discovered, the best options will emerge with the right contextual question and the right bookends to frame it. The question always depends on your company or team's circumstances and situation.

Drawing on the earlier example in Chapter 3, imagine this to be your company's situation:

Cash flow is tight. Business is far from booming. A piece of equipment has become pretty old, and the workers are complaining about it. Customers aren't getting consistent quality.

So an appropriate question would be:

"What is our best near-term option regarding this piece of equipment, considering our tight cash-flow, constrained market, customer quality complaints, and your frustrations with it?"

In the room are John, the team leader; Ben, Jack and Julie, three of his equipment operators; Ralph, the maintenance executive; Audrey, the production planner; and Rick, the overall plant executive.

The CEO starts off with a blank white board. All are happy to be there because the equipment is expensive and all have strong views. The solution affects their sense of achievement. Properly facilitated, an option solving exercise will give them all an opportunity to "buy into" the best option, since a perfect solution is unlikely.

> *Properly facilitated, an option-solving exercise will give participants an opportunity to "buy-in" to the best option.*

All participants are primed with the option solving principles. Remember, there is no discussion about *how, when, why* or *where*. All suggested options are permissible, except the outlandish.

Jack is the first to offer an option. "Completely refit the current machine," he proposes.

Audrey interjects with another option: "Put a double shift on an adjacent machine; then we can decide what to do with this one with more time on our hands."

As everyone starts looking to others for suggestions, John comes up with this: "Let's lease the best machine on the market; then we don't have to find the capital finances right now."

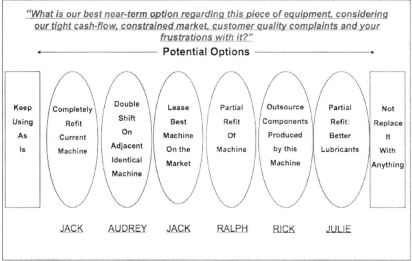

Figure 5   OPTION SOLVING : NOT PROBLEM SOLVING
EXAMPLE 1: OPTION SOLVING

"What is our best near-term option regarding this piece of equipment, considering our tight cash-flow, constrained market, customer quality complaints and your frustrations with it?"

← Potential Options →

| Keep Using As Is | Completely Refit Current Machine | Double Shift On Adjacent Identical Machine | Lease Best Machine On the Market | Partial Refit Of Machine | Outsource Components Produced by this Machine | Partial Refit: Better Lubricants | Not Replace It With Anything |

JACK   AUDREY   JACK   RALPH   RICK   JULIE

Leadership Solutions, Inc.

That inspires Ralph to suggest, "Why don't we do a partial refit of the current machine and replace the most worn parts?"

Everyone is obviously being rather mindful of the cost involved, while cash flow is tight. Rick then jumps in with this idea: "Why don't we outsource these components down the street because Ricky's machine shop can produce items like this pretty easily and at a reasonable cost?"

There's a pause while everyone thinks deeply. All obviously are highly engaged. Julie suggests, as one of the machine's operators: "Why don't we do a partial refit and then use better lubricants, which will reduce wear and tear and keep it running at a cooler temperature – so it will be more reliable."

At this point, everyone seems exhausted of any other ideas, and they look quite pleased with their range of options. Even Ben, who didn't have any suggestions of his own, seemed pretty pleased with the alternatives his colleagues presented. The CEO can see they are all ready to make a choice from the options.

What they decided isn't important here. These are the significant points:

- They did a good job by coming up with six options between the bookends. Experience has shown that if a group doesn't come up with at least five or six key options, it hasn't been imaginative enough.

- By exhausting all the reasonable alternatives, the group will be satisfied with their ultimate choice because they have considered the full range.

- All the participants acted responsibly – even the machine workers. That might surprise some executives, though many others know how mature even shop floor people can be when they are consulted appropriately.

- Although there's an array of option builders, from shop floor worker to senior executive, none is required to come up with a major presentation or launch a debate (both left-brain activities). They can feed off one another's ideas and still be part of the decision flow.

- When the time comes, they will all confidently vote independently on a piece of paper regarding the best option, using their powerful right-brain intuition.

Experience shows that if a group doesn't come up with five or six options, it hasn't been imaginative enough.

Questions for consideration

- To what degree do you put your people on an equal footing when they are involved in resolving important issues?

- To what extent are your facilitation skills good enough to orchestrate an effective outcome?

- To what degree would you allow all the options to come out, without getting bogged down in *how, why, when, where*?

Chapter 6

Second Option Solving Exercise

"'He who hesitates is lost' is one adage the overly cautious CEO should heed. Combining instinct and experience to seize the moment is something just about every CEO needs to do."

-David Dotlich and Peter Cairo, Why CEOs Fail *(Jossey-Bass, 2003)*

C hoice is an important tool to gain emotional buy-in. Smart parents give their willful kids a choice rather than a *fait accompli*: then they usually get cooperation. And though an employee is far from a child, the same principle of human behavior applies. Those who can explore all available choices form an emotional commitment to a solution. If they can picture all the options and visualize what might happen, they will make a more appropriate call. Visualization is more of an intuitive instinct than a rational one.

Those who are allowed to explore various choices become emotionally committed to a solution.

You'll recall the company executive who, in Chapter 3, hoped to improve his leadership team. Here's how the option solving proceeded:

Joe, the president, and Chuck, his CEO, sit with two leadership advisers from outside the company. The advisers know the leadership team well.

Joe and Chuck are eager to move their company forward but feel hampered by the talent and commitment of their team. Joe and Chuck have articulated a bright future, yet they feel the senior team is not incisive and engaged enough to give the company a vital market edge.

Once the foursome formulates the right contextual question ("What's it going to take to get my leadership team more involved?") and establish the bookends ("Continue treading water with the same team" vs. "Throw in the towel and sell the company"), Chuck offers this idea: "Why not immediately change leaders? There are two, in my opinion, who are holding the team back."

The names and specifics are not mentioned. Under the principles of good option solving, it is more important at this point to flush out the various options rather than focus on the details of one.

One of the advisers suggests: "Reorganize the company around its key leadership talent, such that the less ineffectual members would be repositioned into roles more suited to their talent level."

The other adviser asks: "Is there a particular crisis that's about to emerge that everyone can rally around, or something else that would suffice as a 'call to action'?" He reasons that a crisis could encourage people to step up to the plate. Neither Joe nor Chuck respond, either in words or body language, so the discussion moves on.

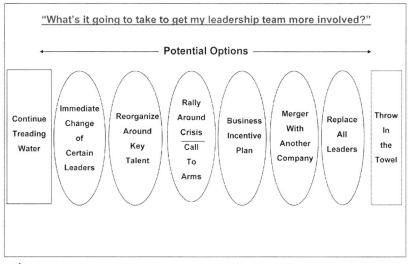

Figure 6

OPTION SOLVING : NOT PROBLEM SOLVING
EXAMPLE 2: OPTION SOLVING

"What's it going to take to get my leadership team more involved?"

Potential Options

| Continue Treading Water | Immediate Change of Certain Leaders | Reorganize Around Key Talent | Rally Around Crisis Call To Arms | Business Incentive Plan | Merger With Another Company | Replace All Leaders | Throw In the Towel |

Leadership Solutions, Inc.

©1994-2009 Leadership Solutions. Inc. ® (MALRC) All rights reserved.

Joe then suggests, "Maybe we should come up with a business incentive plan and set certain key objectives over the next 12 months, with a bonus pool at the end." He can see from the look in his advisers' eyes that they wouldn't favor that. They see incentives as satisfiers, not motivators. (See Fred Herzberg's seminal work in this area, *Motivation-Hygiene Theory*.) Besides, the group had talked about this idea a few times before in the past year. The consensus was that it was akin to lighting fires under people rather than within them. If the incentive were removed, people would just go back to old habits.

Chuck suggests this: "Maybe we could merge with Company XYZ. They have some good leaders which could create a good combined team." The look on Joe's face isn't exactly encouraging, even though he is working hard to come up with another alternative.

He also looks at his two advisers and thinks about a recent discussion regarding the merger idea. All had agreed then that a merger was out of the question unless 1) a company has the leadership strength to sustain it (Joe clearly didn't have that confidence); and 2) a company has the financial strength and resources to cope (Joe doubted it); and 3) there is a good cultural fit.

On that final point, Joe felt a merger should be like marrying an oak tree to a smaller oak tree – not to a fir tree. He believed a merger with XYZ would amount to the latter.

Finally, one of the leadership advisers proposes this: "What about replacing all the leadership team over time? I would only suggest doing it over a staged period of time, since it would be overly disruptive to handle all at once." It is duly noted as another option, while all present start looking at one another for further possibilities.

Again, there is no discussion about the *how, why, when* or *where* of any of these options. But a shaking and nodding of heads is enough to indicate that participants are satisfied with the range of options and have no others to propose.

Taking a restroom or coffee break for about 10 minutes is a pretty good approach for allowing people to distance themselves from the choices.

At that moment, Joe suggests that everyone take a restroom or coffee break for about 10 minutes. Such an approach is good for allowing people the opportunity to distance themselves from the choices. This is known as "emotional distancing," which will be discussed in detail in Chapter 8.

Ten minutes later, when the group reconvenes, Joe asks everyone if they want to make any comments about the potential options or if anyone has come up with others. Nobody speaks up. So he asks everyone, "What option seems to make the most sense in light of our current situation?" and asks them to write their responses on scraps of paper for a tally.

He collects them quickly and reveals a unanimous preference for "immediate change of certain leaders." The group members immediately begin pouring out why they favor that option. Here are their thoughts:

- If the two people mentioned by Chuck are changed, it will signal to others that Joe is serious about expecting good leadership from everyone on the team.

- Neither of the two is viewed as a strong team player.

- A strong contender exists to fill the spot of one of them. The other one's talents could be used elsewhere in the company, if the person will accept a different reward package.

- It is the least disruptive option, though the others have merit. Done properly, it will aid momentum.

All the participants feel emotionally comfortable because they have considered all the most reasonable options.

The option solvers felt emotionally comfortable with the decision because they had considered all reasonable choices.

Option solving with larger groups

When option solving involves more than a few people, recommended practices will change. If you are working with a board of, say, thirty people, allow about half a day, as opposed to two or three hours for five to ten people, until fully familiar with this approach. In addition, do the following:

- Before the session, prepare an appropriate contextual question with the meeting sponsors. Later, give the full group an opportunity to ratify or adjust the question.

- For the uninitiated, give the group a quick overview of what option solving is all about.

- Brief the participants on the challenge to be resolved.

- Separate them into subgroups of four to six people. Each subgroup should include people with differing backgrounds or interests.

- Ask each subgroup to consider the question and come up with one or two ideas for a set of bookends. After discussion, ask the subgroups for any adjustments to the contextual question, and then hear their bookend suggestions. List those suggestions for all to see. The participants as a whole can now vote for the most likely set of bookends. Once they are chosen, again these are drawn up on a white board for all to see.

- Invite the subgroups to each come up with at least two options that fit between the bookends.

- Don't let the subgroup discussions go on too long, or they may get bogged down in minutia and lose creativity. Establish how much time the subgroups will have, and warn them not to get sidetracked on issues involving *how, why, when* and *where.* The facilitator should look out for such behavior or ask each group to appoint a watchdog.

- After the subgroups report their options, list them for everyone to see. From this listing, the facilitator can draw upon the collective right-brain wisdom of the participants to pickout five or six most likely options – see *The Wisdom of Crowds* by James Surowiecki (Anchor Books-Random House, 2004, 2005).

- Now, conduct a confidential vote. Ask each person to write the option they favor on a piece of paper, and collect the votes. A consensus will likely emerge, although the more people involved, the more likely it will be that votes are spread across several options. If that happens, give the group a five- to ten-minute break and encourage participants to talk to one another about the top choices.

- At the end of that "emotional-distancing" break, request a new confidential poll focusing on the choices that got the most votes. One option likely will emerge as the clear preference.

Questions for Consideration

- If you are the principle executive of a company, to what degree do you invite the right group of people to resolve a particular issue?

- To what degree do you allow for "emotional distancing" after a brainstorming session?

- What time do you normally allow for all reasonable possibilities to emerge?

Chapter 7

* *

Peeling the Onion

"A(n insurance) carrier's business processes are much like the layers of an onion. If you peel back enough of them, you eventually get to the core."

-Robert Regis Hayle, "Techdecisions," Journal for Insurance,

November 2008

P rofessionals often use the metaphor of peeling an onion to get down to the best answer to a question, whether they are detectives, research scientists or art historians. And most of us use the concept unconsciously when resolving an issue in our lives: We think about it, come to a conclusion, and then think about what underlies our conclusion. It's a universal idea – and option solving uses it to its best.

To illustrate, let's consider a pressing issue for a service-oriented business: How to develop client commitment from the start. There are three types of clients: new ones, ones being cultivated, and committed ones.

The company – let's call it WXY – obviously wants committed clients who are satisfied with services and products, make good references, pay on time, and are loyal to the brand. A customer-oriented company should have at least 20 percent of clients in that category. Good companies do much better and have four or five criteria to intuitively define who is committed.

"Cultivational" clients are those not yet committed. In most companies, a significant number of clients fall into that category. They may have been dissatisfied with products or services at the outset, or there was not a good fit between client and provider. The company may be inept at providing products or services that meet their real needs. The client may feel neglected, or just need more time. There can be many reasons. Often such clients say, "We did not experience what we expected when we made our buying decision," and they no longer bring their full purchasing power to the provider.

Such is the case with company WXY. It has decided to place a much greater emphasis on moving clients from "new" to "committed" as quickly as possible. It decides to do so by striving to treat them properly at the outset.

WXY assembles a team of six: Ron, the operations team leader; Grace, the client services team leader; Judy and Dick from within those two teams; and Carol and Andy from other WXY groups. Grace is nominated to be facilitator for their option solving exercise.

She and Ron "set the stage" for the team so that it understands the client categories (new, cultivational, and committed) and WXY's determination to improve and grow. They explain the team's imperative: Determine the best way forward and recommend it to the executives for their approval. The team agrees its purpose is to answer the question, "What approach will enable us to build committed clients from the outset?"

Grace challenges the team to determine a set of bookends. The group talks awhile and agrees on these: 1) Keep the current inconsistency, or 2) Make radical changes. Within that framework, the participants rapidly move to find options.

Dick quickly suggests: "Why don't we beef up both the client services and operations teams, so they are better equipped for doing their job?" Other team members sense his level of irritation at WXY's lack of responsiveness in that regard.

Ron proposes: "We should probably form a new, appropriately staffed implementation team that can get the job done within three months."

There are a few nods around the room, especially after Judy suggests: "I believe WXY should enhance the leadership strength of both current teams." A few people, fearing that Grace and Ron will be embarrassed, squirm in their seats. However, Grace says: "I believe we need some intense training for both the client services and operations teams."

A few people squirmed in their seats, fearing that Grace and Ron would be embarrassed.

Dick jumps in again: "I believe another option is to merge operations and client services into multipurpose teams, where they can implement and meet ongoing client service and operation needs."

"I was thinking along the same lines," offers Andy who had been pretty quiet.

Everyone now looks toward Carol for her suggestion. "I can't think of any other alternatives right now. I'm pretty comfortable with all the options you guys have picked."

Figure 7   **OPTION SOLVING : NOT PROBLEM SOLVING**

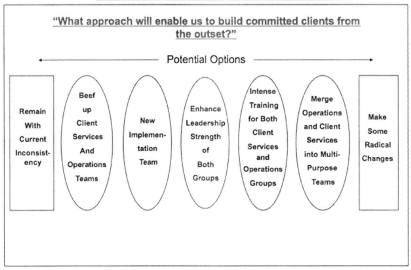

Grace can see that everyone else feels pretty much the same way, so she invites everyone to write down their preferred option, prompted by the question, "What option seems to make the most sense in light of our current situation?"

As they do this, Ron requests a five-minute break, while Grace counts the tally. When everyone returns, she declares that four had opted for "forming a new implementation team" and two had opted for "intense training for both client services and operations teams." This provokes a healthy discussion.

After some debate, Grace asks, "So what do we think? Do we focus on forming a new implementation team or some intense training for client services and operations teams?"

"Well, if I knew how we intended to go about forming a new implementation team, I may be willing to go along with that option," interjects Carol, obviously one of those who voted for intense training. "I will go along with that," adds Judy, who also had favored training.

The Peeling Begins

"Okay then," replies Grace, "why don't we peel back the onion and figure out what options we have in forming a new implementation team?" Everyone nods.

Grace refocuses the team on defining the question, "What would be the best way of forming a strong implementation team?" along with two further new bookends. The team comes up with these 1) Let it evolve over time, or 2) Use outside consultants to recommend and build.

Everyone's right brains kicked in as they began comparing options.

Since neither of those options is tenable to the participants, they seem to be a good starting point. Everyone's right brains kick in as they begin making comparisons with the emerging picture on the flip chart.

Andy breaks the silence: "Why don't we pick the best implementers from both the operations and client services team and pull them together into a new implementation team?" This creates an interesting starting point. Carol says: "Why don't we ask for volunteers who wish to participate in such a team, from across the company?"

More silence follows as everyone turns their creative minds on. Dick offers: "Why don't we hire some new hotshots from our competitors to form a totally fresh team, with fresh ideas?"

"That's an interesting idea, Dick," says Ron, "but I think we could appoint a duo of two team leaders, one from operations and one from customer services, and let them pick a team."

Judy suddenly becomes energized: "I know: Why don't we form a Cyber-Age Team with 21st-century team roles?"

Everyone looks at her as if she's coming from outerspace. "A friend of mine," she continues, "is working at a company where it has established one or two of these teams: the most important thing being that everyone on the team has a distinct role to play."

"For instance, my friend was telling me that a technical software team had been formed and, instead of everyone on the team being just software engineers, where everyone would usually listen to the most experienced person in the room, everyone was given a distinct role to play."

"She told me about roles such as 'dreamers,' those out-of-the-box thinkers from their skunk works; or 'conceptualizers,' the software-architects and application-oriented people; or 'coders,' the software protocol writers; or 'beta operators,' who are software-testers and de-buggers; or 'developers' who fine tune and maintain the software."

Everyone is listening wide-eyed as Judy continues: "Of course, they have a team leader appointed by the team, with their IT group executive's blessing, who is responsible for the "bigger picture" thinking and is the coach-mentor and orchestrator-coordinator of the team. My understanding is that the team has become a dynamic force within the company."

She pauses and then comments, "It would be interesting to see us form an implementation team with fresh roles."

There's a pregnant pause as the option solvers absorb this startling idea. Some are thinking: "Wow, Judy, you normally sit at your desk and get on with your work; we don't often hear ideas from you like this!" Perhaps, they wonder, she's never had a forum to make such interesting contributions.

After a few moments, Grace comments, "Well, I'm at a loss to suggest any more options, so I'd be quite comfortable choosing from any of these. Does anyone else have any more alternatives?" Everyone shakes their heads.

"So why don't we take a ten minute break and then we'll make our choice," she says. (That, as we shall see in the next chapter, is to allow "emotional distancing.") The room fills with the rattle of chairs being pushed back and the buzz of conversation, much of it with Judy.

We don't need to stay for the team's choice. What's important here is how the group "peeled the onion" to discover new solutions. In fact, the team could very well peel it further, delving ever deeper beneath the surface and finding options within options.

When people are free to put their imaginations to
work, they make amazing contributions.

Other important points are these: By "peeling the onion" and further discussing the issues, Carol and Judy were pulled onto the majority's side without feeling uncomfortable or pressured. And Judy was able to introduce a totally fresh idea, the cyber-age team. When imaginations are free to work – when the right brain gets an opportunity – people make amazing contributions.

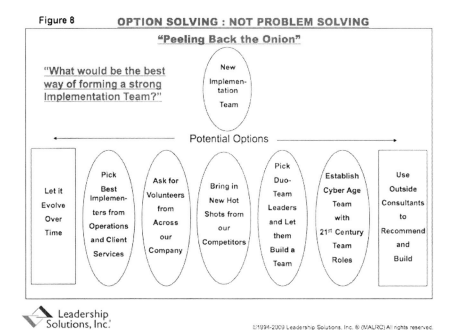

Figure 8 — OPTION SOLVING : NOT PROBLEM SOLVING — "Peeling Back the Onion"

Questions for consideration

- To what degree do you allow your people the opportunity to introduce free-form ideas in a "safe" forum?

- To what degree do people in your organization "peel back the onion" to resolve key issues?

- What do you think would be the advantages of "peeling the onion" on issues affecting your organization?

Chapter 8

Emotional Distancing

"Dicks has grappled with all manner of complex legal and financial issues while wandering in the Land of Nod, but he says his most vital sleepwork has been strategic – how to structure his businesses, which markets to invade and conquer, to know when to take a calculated risk."

- Anne Fisher, "Make Sleep Work for You," Fortune

Small Business, September 2008

S uccessful people emotionally distance themselves from issues by making good use of sleep, naps and breaks. During quiet time, they find they can use their intuitive gifts to realize the best options.

Instead of forcing ourselves to consciously analyze an issue, we can let the unconscious mind do much of the work for which it is so well equipped. During sleep (in particular) or break time, the left brain is less likely to be firing questions at the right brain for answers. Hence, the right brain can relax and get to work on the challenging, complex issues that need answers when we wake.

Such forms of emotional distancing help us make better overall decisions and are therefore important to society. The time out is not for analyzing and researching for hours, though both activities can be useful. It is a time to relax, to let the intuitive mind work in a natural way. Crossword puzzle addicts know that when they get stuck for a word, it often pops into their mind if they get away for a few hours.

Emotional distancing is not time out for analyzing and researching. It is a time to relax and let the intuitive mind work naturally.

Let's look at an option solving example that illustrates emotional distancing:

A company leadership team has just completed an off-site session where it formulated a compelling vision. It was determined to communicate the vision to every corner of the organization. Two of the team members agree to act as sponsors of such an initiative. They are Mary, who leads the product engineering team, and Sammy, who leads the company's research and development efforts. They get four others at different levels of the company to join them: Greg, a shift leader; Jack, from inventory; Keith, a senior machine operator; and Mark, from product development.

In a session facilitated by an outsider, they consider some immediate and ongoing options. They know that to fully get the vision message across, they will probably have to touch most people in the company repeatedly in quite different ways. *(Note: My experience has shown that to get people's complete attention, you have to reach them through at least six diverse methods: for example, newspaper article, radio announcement, TV bulletin, billboard, bus sign, a big blimp overhead.)*

The team quickly establishes an appropriate question: "What would be the most effective means of communicating the company's vision?"

And it establishes these bookends:

Take the usual ad-hoc approach. As in most companies, communicating the vision would be left to happenstance as it winds its way through the organization.

Don't bother at all. The leadership team would keep a tight hold on the reins and keep the vision to itself. Implausible? Many companies keep their people in the dark, sometimes because the executives themselves don't know where they're going. It's called "mushroom management" (because mushrooms grow in the dark and 'management' because managers typically keep too much close to their vest), characterized by employees complaining about a lack of communication.

Since the team members do not wish to take either of these roads, they start to consider their range of options.

Mary speaks up first: "Let's re-launch the company's newsletter." Most team members seem to have liked the former newsletter. The facilitator mentions that newsletters should include mainly pictures and stories as much as possible, to engage the right brain, rather than just dissertations for the left brain.

Greg next proposes: "Why don't we hold a series of company events, besides the annual picnic and holiday party, to focus on the themes of the vision?"

Keith jumps in with, "Let's flash messages and Intranet bulletins on people's computer screens on the shop floor and around the company." That idea, too, seems to be received enthusiastically.

Mark offers: "Let's sponsor an in-house road show, where Kyle [the CEO] and the senior leadership team can meet with all groups in the company to talk about the vision."

That prompts Sammy to quickly suggest: "Let's orchestrate some quarterly town hall meetings, so that whoever wishes to attend can hear updates directly from the senior leadership team and ask any pertinent questions." There are a few nods of approval for the idea.

And finally Jack throws in this option: "Let's send out information bulletins with people's paychecks." He says he's heard a number of companies have been doing that for years.

Figure 9 **OPTION SOLVING : NOT PROBLEM SOLVING**

"What would be the most effective means of communicating the company's vision?"

← ———————— Potential Options ———————— →

Usual Ad-hoc Approach	Re-launch Newsletter (Using Pictures and stories)	Series Of Company Events	In-house Road Show	Intranet And Media	Town Hall Meetings	Pay-Check Notes	Not Bother at all
	MARY	GREG	MARK	KEITH	SAMMY	JACK	

Leadership Solutions, Inc.®
Insightful Solutions for Effective Leadership Performance

As the options are presented, the facilitator draws them up on a white board for all to see. *(NOTE: In the accompanying chart, each idea is marked with the name of who offered it, to assist the reader. However, in a live option solving session, it isn't helpful to tie people's names to any chart; in fact, they may be reluctant to contribute in the future if they feel they are to be labeled forever with a particular spontaneous idea.)*

At this point, the facilitator can see that team members are happy with their options and have no more to offer. The participants write down their choices. Jack and Greg balk a little because they want more time to consider the options.

"Does everyone want to take a ten-minute break?" the facilitator asks. Mary and Sammy stand up to acknowledge the opportunity, and the facilitator suggests that people not analyze or discuss their thoughts too much while out of the room. Ten minutes later, everyone is back from the "emotional distancing" break.

The facilitator again asks everyone to write down their choice and submit it. When the facilitator takes score, three have chosen 'Series of company events' and three have chosen 'In-house road show'. There are smiles all around, followed by comments on how tough a choice it was. Still, all agree it's important to pick the right option.

The facilitator suggests that they sleep on it, and requests that participants ask themselves this question just before bedtime: "What option will give us the biggest lift in getting the word out on the vision?" Upon awakening, the facilitator tells them, they should write down the first intuitive choice that surfaces, then meet together in the canteen for a quick cup of coffee upon arriving at work.

The next morning, Mark and Keith arrive first, quickly followed by the others. Without any prior discussion, everyone hands over their votes to Mary. She tallies them to find five votes for the road show and one for the company events.

They were invited to write down the first choice that surfaced when they woke, and then meet for coffee when they arrived at work.

Jack declares that he's the one still in favor of the company events but is comfortable going along with the majority.

With that, all agree to getting together two days later to discuss how to orchestrate the road show. They all appear quite comfortable with the chosen option.

The calming effect of emotional distancing can be amazing. It greatly helps a group arrive at a consensus – even for someone like Jack who had clearly thought differently. He seemed satisfied that everyone had been heard and had given due deliberation to their final choice.

Questions for consideration

- Consider where you have used emotional distancing in your work life on more than one occasion. What were the ultimate outcomes of that?

- What has been one of the more difficult business or organizational decisions you have had to make over the past year? Did you use emotional distancing as part of that decision?

- What do you see as the key differences between time spent on rational analysis and emotional distancing?

Chapter 9

Our Biases and Expertise

"It is particularly hard for people to make good decisions when they have trouble translating the choices they face into experiences they will have."
-From Nudge, *Thaler and Sunstein (Penguin Books, 2008)*

The above quote, from "Nudge" by Richard Thaler and Cass Sunstein, and the book itself bring two important issues to mind when making the most from option solving:

- Our biases when making judgments about a whole host of things.

- Being properly informed about or experienced in the issues when choosing options.

Nudge reminds us of the many cultural and personal biases that we are likely to have. These include:

Rules of thumb. We use simple rules of thumb to help us make guesstimates to move things along. However, within these rules of thumb there are opportunities for personal biases – for example, Americans generally think their European counterparts are culturally superior, sophisticated and quite genteel. That view overlooks the greater percentage of Europeans who are working-class, everyday people. Go to a European football game – Americans call it soccer – and see for yourself.

> *Executives are often right in their hunches about their people, but they can be wrong, too. They must be ready for exceptions.*

We are full of other stereotypes, especially in the workplace. Executives are often right in their hunches about people within their organization, but they can also be wrong, too – based upon people's academics, or the way they present themselves, or the way they articulate points of view. We have to be ready for the exceptions, of which there are so many.

Over-optimism. There's clearly more to be gained by being optimistic than pessimistic. Effective leaders aim to be as optimistic as possible, but their credibility wanes when staff think they are unrealistic. Most teams and individuals are likely to perceive themselves better than they really are. Most of us see ourselves as better than the average person, even when our work is clearly not up to par. Also, we will tend to block out the pessimists because we believe they are just being negative, when in fact they may have a valid point of view.

Winning. We love to be on the winning side. We don't like to talk about our losses. We are prone to seeing ourselves as better than our competitors. But in fact, when we underestimate our competitors we are more likely to lose.

Status quo. Most of us are strongly inclined to stick with our current situation rather than move right along. It seems to takes society about thirty years to fully adopt something new. When you look back at many inventions, it seems to take them a generation or more to become mainstream. Status quo and inertia are around us all the time.

It seems to take a generation or more for an invention to become mainstream.

Herd mentality. Often we seem to find it difficult not to follow the mob. We become lemmings. We wear a particular style of suit or dress because many others are doing so. Because our executives do not particularly focus on the customer, we accept behaviors that are not as friendly to customers as they should be.

Temptation. Organizations are full of temptations, such as opportunities to take the easy way out. Or we may be tempted to think of our bosses as great leaders when in fact so many are not. We may find ourselves taking office supplies home so we don't have to buy our own pens and pencils. We may be tempted to keep our own star shining by scoring political points against others. A team trying to advance its proposals might "sock it" to another team, or department.

A smart option solving facilitator will be aware of such human biases. It is wise to invite a fairly diverse group to participate in option solving exercises: senior and junior staff, optimists and less optimistic souls, those who are politically astute and those who are less so. Such precautions will help minimize the high risk of biases in the selection of a final option.

And as noted earlier in this book, votes during option solving should be done anonymously, on folded slips of paper. That reduces the chance of participants' going with the herd. If a bias arises, the meeting facilitator should immediately challenge it because when other participants are aware of bias in the room, they become less satisfied with the outcome of the exercise.

> *When participants are aware of bias in the room,*
> *they become less satisfied with the outcome*
> *of the exercise.*

Ensuring participants have sufficient expertise

Option solving teams cannot be expected to produce the best solutions when they don't have the expertise to do so. They should have the opportunity to invite an expert to join them when necessary. Also, team members should be encouraged to read up on particular topics to prepare themselves for an exercise. (Note: An expert can advise the group on what information to read.)

A facilitator needs to give participants appropriate background briefings. After the briefing, participants can use their organizational wisdom and their intuition to synthesize all the complexities involved in making the right call. Quite naturally, if the issue relates to something within their company, there's a good chance participants already have a good feel for the situation. On the other hand, if it is something on the outside, they are less likely to be properly informed – and more likely to fall back on their biases.

> *In the absence of solid insights, people are likely to*
> *fall back onto their biases.*

However, it's best to avoid the delays that surveys or studies would cause. They probably won't add much to the overall picture, and they kill momentum. If such information gathering seems useful, perhaps it could be done before the option solving session begins so that participants have the data available at the outset.

The painful "gulf" in communication (The vacuum for bias)

In many companies, executives tend to communicate in one language and the workforce in another. Executives tend to communicate in financial terms, whereas their workforces tend to talk about fair treatment, recognition for achievements, job security, good relationships, and more. By their very nature, executives and employees have biases and perceptions about each other.

Executives tend to communicate in financial terms,
and workforces tend to talk about personal issues.

That often is manifested in finger pointing and stalemates. The bigger the organization, the bigger is the issue; it's particularly pronounced in large, traditional organizations. It culminates in executives distrusting the choices of their workforces because they are not couched in the financial jargon to which executives are accustomed. The workers distrust the choices of their executives, citing the financial jargon that seems to signal a lack of empathy with their issues.

An executive might respond like this, for example: "We have made a business decision not to pursue your requests…." But the words "business decision" imply to the workers that the executive cares more about the owners and shareholders than about the workforce.

*To workforces, the executives' financial jargon can
seem like a foreign language that signals a
lack of empathy.*

In India, where many company programs have been outsourced since the mid-'90s, executives have increasingly embraced English as their language, even among one another. Their workforces continue to communicate in their local languages and dialects, of which there are many hundreds. They don't understand English. There's a growing schism in communication between elite executives and their workers.

Likewise, when Western executives talk financial jargon, it may seem like a foreign language to the workforce. It can increase the gulf between them. Workforces may see bias toward the ownership. Executives may suspect that choices made by the workforce are self-serving.

It's important, therefore, that executives and workforces discuss their biases and "language" as part of any option solving exercise. If they do, the choices they make through their collective wisdom are more likely to gain acceptance and action. (Note: "Collective wisdom," which reflects both independent thinking and the "intuitive whole," is an important concept in option solving. It's the synthesis of many "whole minds" and the insights of diverse groups.)

Questions for consideration

- To what extent do you take advantage of the collective wisdom in your organization?

- What sort of gulf do you observe that is created by different "languages" within your organization?

- To what degree do you perceive biases creeping into decisions and choices in your organization?

- To what extent do you expose decision makers to expert resources before asking them to choose options?

Chapter 10

The Way Forward

"It is the nature of man to rise to greatness,
if greatness is expected of him."
-John Steinbeck (Grapes Of Wrath)

Option solving is a more natural and engaging
approach than problem solving, which is a rational
and tedious process.

As we look forward to how option solving can lead us to smart decisions, let's review what we have learned about its many advantages. Here's what it can do for you and your company:

- Takes full advantage of people's "whole-mind" and its capabilities, particularly the powerful intuitive mind and its superior judgment based upon living and experience.

- Promotes forward momentum rather than letting issues become bogged down in indecision. This not only saves time and money but it also quickly capitalizes on important opportunities. It uses the momentum of emotion without becoming side tracked with analysis, surveys and research.

- Moves people away from problem solving, a generally rational and tedious process, toward something more natural, engaging and superior.

- Takes advantage of several perspectives simultaneously rather than just one or two, thereby challenging participants to break free from their biases and traditional lines of thought.

- Explores all reasonable possibilities, thereby putting the right brain at ease and minimizing the uncertainty so often created when the intuitive mind is dissatisfied with the usual limited choices coming out of traditional problem solving.

- Allows people to be much more creative in finding solutions to issues, rather than getting bogged down in the typical, depressing "what's wrong" approach of problem solving.

- Overcomes the possibility of participants deferring to the most seasoned person in the room for setting the pace, since all participants are on a level playing field at the outset and everyone's contributions are welcome.

- Encourages the use of an initial framework (the right contextual question and bookends) to stimulate people's intuitive capabilities and retain their focus.

- Uses the concept of "peeling the onion" to find multi-level solutions to more complex issues.

- Makes good use of "emotional distancing," enabling people's intuitions to work at their best.

- Permits a wider involvement of company staff, instilling a feeling of stronger communication.

- Does not require participants to be highly sophisticated presenters, debaters or articulate thinkers, since it draws primarily upon their experience and intuition.

- Provides the opportunity for facilitators to hone their leadership skills, even if they are not yet appointed leaders.

- Is usually likely to be an engaging and energizing experience.

- Can be used in sales scenarios to steer prospects or customers toward the best solutions to meet business needs.

- Increases the possibility of inspirational moments, which can often produce breakthroughs.

- Helps to deal with "naysayers" who will try to find holes in anything unless it suits their purpose.

Option solving is useful in sales scenarios to steer prospects or customers toward the best solutions.

For professional and personal use

Let's look at one more example to illustrate the value of option solving and how it can help move forward not just a company, but the individuals within.

Paul is an experienced senior salesperson. He realizes that a sales colleague, John, is intruding on some of his key prospects. Paul is angry at John's unfair behavior.

Paul sits down with an option solving facilitator to share his feelings and explore all his options. The process also helps him to calm down. They clarify the question: "What could be the most effective way to address his colleague?" And they come up with a set of bookends: 1) Leave things as they are, or 2) Have a bust-up with John.

These nicely set a reality framework for Paul. He is now in a position to explore all his intermediary options. His first idea is, "Try to reason with John." And then, after a pause, "I could discuss the situation with Eric." Eric, the company president, is not always easily reachable because of his schedule.

The facilitator suggests, "Meet with both John and Eric to discuss the situation."

Paul keeps thinking. To prod things along, the facilitator adds: "Talk it through with Rick after two or three weeks." Rick is the new vice president for sales; he was the replacement for a sales executive who left several weeks earlier, so letting a few weeks pass would give Rick time to establish himself before reviewing Paul's issue.

Then Paul comes out with this: "Why not invite John to lunch, so I can discuss how we can negotiate this?" This seems to be the option Paul is looking for, as he immediately starts relating all the advantages of handling it that way.

Figure 10   **OPTION SOLVING : NOT PROBLEM SOLVING**

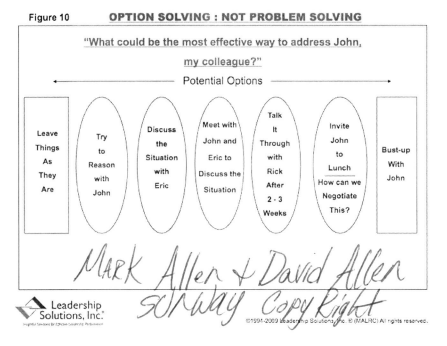

"What could be the most effective way to address John, my colleague?"

Potential Options

| Leave Things As They Are | Try to Reason with John | Discuss the Situation with Eric | Meet with John and Eric to Discuss the Situation | Talk It Through with Rick After 2 - 3 Weeks | Invite John to Lunch How can we Negotiate This? | Bust-up With John |

That example shows how option solving can be brought to bear for individual issues or dilemmas, too. It's what a vast majority of people do, instinctively, but it formalizes such an approach so that individuals reap more value from it, with out-of-the-box options and solutions. It provides a more formal technique to elicit optimum solutions at a particular moment in time.

In Paul's case, the exercise empowered him to perceive his best option at the moment and immediately made him feel much more at ease with his situation. He could now see, through his own deliberations, a positive way forward. The fact that he considered all reasonable options made him that much more comfortable with his ultimate choice. His choice to have lunch with John gave him the confidence to try to resolve this issue himself, rather than involve

Option solving empowered him to see his best option at the moment, and it immediately helped him to feel at ease.

senior leaders and creating a risk of alienation. It also gave him a friendly way to signal to John that his behavior was not acceptable.

Example of famous intuitive thinkers

Though we are inclined to value our classical training in rational problem solving, history gives us striking examples of people who seem to have thrived through intuitive thinking.

Consider the life and times of Cornelius Vanderbilt, one of the first genuine American moguls. According to *The First Tycoon*, by T. J. Stiles (Alfred A. Knopf, 2009), Vanderbilt was born on Staten Island, New York, to a modest farming family. He attended school for only a few months, contemptuous of "written English," according to the author. He began working on ferries and schooners in the 1820s and '30s.

Vanderbilt pursued many right choices and options, probably using his intuition rather than more classical problem solving methods.

By the time he was about 50, "nearly everyone who traveled between Boston and New York took a Vanderbilt boat or train." He is still well known for the building of Grand Central Station. "If he had been able to sell all his assets at full market value at the moment of his death … he would have taken one out of every twenty dollars in circulation," Stiles wrote. Vanderbilt must have pursued many of the right choices and options, probably using his intuition rather than more classical problem solving methods.

To name but a few others, consider these successfull individuals who shunned a more classical education : Albert Einstein, Bill Gates (Microsoft), Richard Branson (Virgin Atlantic Airways), Winston Churchill, Charles Schwab, and John Harrison. The latter was an uneducated English carpenter of the 18th century who invented the marine chronometer, which revolutionized world navigation.

Some of them were considered dyslexic, possibly because their rational minds were not equipped to work in classical ways. Perhaps all of them relied on their hunches or intuitions instead; and even though many of them were in the right place at the right time, they took advantage of their best options.(See Malcolm Gladwell's book *Outliers*, Little, Brown and Company, 2008). This gives all of us hope that pursuing our intuitions, aided by option solving, will lead us and our organizations to the most opportunities.

The example of such highly successful people gives us hope that pursuing our intuitions will lead to the most opportunities.

Nothing ventured…

Venture capitalists, by definition, look to the future. But they pay virtually no attention to the business plans of small companies that they are thinking of investing in.

"Because they make decisions 'under conditions of high uncertainty,' venture capitalists rely on instinct and their expertise in ferreting out information by other means to evaluate the prospects of a business," Brent Bowers reported in a *New York Times* small business article in May 2009 titled "Investors Pay Business Plans Little Heed, Study Finds."

Venture capitalists pay scant attention to materials provided by entrepreneurs, the article pointed out, reporting on a study. Nor do they look at the executive team "lineup," or an entrepreneur's prior start-up experiences or prior success in raising capital.

"In general, business plans don't matter. Nobody is going to read them," said one of the study's authors, Brent Goldfarb, associate professor of management and entrepreneurship at Robert H. Smith School of Business at the University of Maryland, who was quoted in the article. It did encourage entrepreneurs to create business plans anyway so that they would think issues through. It recommended creating a business plan as a "useful warm-up exercise for getting through the venture capitalists' door."

Move from easy to tough issues. That builds confidence and momentum to tackle the ones most challenging.

Next steps toward smart decisions

Going forward, companies and individuals should list all the issues that can potentially stymie them. Prioritize those issues, and then start picking them off one by one with the use of option solving.

Start with one of your easier issues, then work toward tougher ones. That way, you'll build confidence, and momentum. You'll build a head of steam before tackling the most challenging issues.

It is now likely that, in a relatively short time, you will see real progress under way. You'll be a much calmer and confident leader, to boot. You'll have learned how option solving makes the best use of the extraordinary capabilities of the human mind. No problem.

Final questions for consideration

- What will be the key ultimate advantages for you in option solving?

- What pressing personal or professional issue could you resolve today through option solving?

- To what extent are you prepared to seriously practice option solving until it becomes a habit that gains you a reputation of being a terrific decision maker?

- To what extent will you use this technique as a leader so that those around you will admire the way you involve them in decision making?

For more Option Solving examples and talk, please go to:
www.OptionSolving.com.

Author's Final Point

Many will consider the outcomes/options you produce to be just common sense. "Big deal!" they might say. "We don't need an outsider to tell us that!" The truth is, what is obvious in hindsight is often invisible in foresight.

The options all seem so "logical." That is the trap. All good ideas are logical in hindsight – if the idea isn't logical and rational, we would never appreciate its value. However, just because the idea is logical in hindsight doesn't mean it would have been accessible to logic in foresight. Using logic (e.g., problem solving, analysis, etc.) cannot give us fresh, new ideas; it normally only makes corrections or improvements on what already exists.

Our human minds need provocation to break out of their track and view things from a fresh perspective. In history, provocations for great inventions and discoveries have been provided by chance, accident, mistake, confluence of circumstances, madness, and many other sources. But we do not have to await such things – we can deliberately use provocations to create fresh perspectives. (Interestingly, since inventions are always so "logical" in hindsight, it is rare for the inventor to spend much time explaining "how" the discovery was made, as opposed to what the discovery involved. For example, Tiffany was known to add small amounts of gold in crafting his famous art glass. Few actually know that when his gold ring slipped off into a vat of molten glass, he was mesmerized with the beautiful color; subsequently, he figured out precise amounts of gold to add for special affects.)

The beauty of option solving is that it enables problem solving and creative thinking to occur rapidly. It combines our intuitive intelligence (massive amount of information stored in our brains which often cannot be verbalized or even made conscious) with provocation that causes instant insight, a sudden realization: Ah-ha!

Sometimes groups or individuals conclude their option solving activity with the same intuitive outcome as they had going into it. But that's great! It means the exercise confirmed their original intuitive decision. They can proceed with few qualms, grateful they have verified their instinctual choice.

Thanks, Jeff.

A note to facilitators: At the outset of option solving, encourage participants to note how they feel about the issue at hand: Unsure or confused? Lost for ideas? Unhappy about the situation? Later, when the final option emerges, they can refer back to their original state of mind. They can genuinely say, "Ah-ha!"

Index (with chapters indicated)

TreeNeutral

Advantage Media Group is proud to be a part of the Tree Neutral™ program. Tree Neutral offsets the number of trees consumed in the production and printing of this book by taking proactive steps such as planting trees in direct proportion to the number of trees used to print books. To learn more about Tree Neutral, please visit www.treeneutral. com. To learn more about Advantage Media Group's commitment to being a responsible steward of the environment, please visit www. advantagefamily.com/green

---

LaVergne, TN USA
15 April 2010
179422LV00007B/51/P